When Jesus Did His Miracles Of Love

Words by Norman C. Habel
Pictures by Jim Roberts

A PURPLE PUZZLE TREE BOOK

COPYRIGHT © 1973 CONCORDIA PUBLISHING HOUSE, ST. LOUIS, MISSOURI

MANUFACTURED IN THE UNITED STATES OF AMERICA
ALL RIGHTS RESERVED
ISBN 0-570-06541-0

Concordia Publishing House

Would you like to take a trip with me
to the land where Jesus wandered?
Would you like to take a walk with me
down the roads where He went walking?
Would you like to see His miracles
for people just like you?

Then follow me;
we're off to see
some miracles of love.
They bring new joys
to girls and boys,
that come from heaven above.

The first surprise
when you open your eyes
is a man who looks like others.
His clothes are worn,
but His eyes are warm,
and the beggars are His brothers.

Look!
A leper is running down the road,
rushing down the mountainside.
"Unclean! Unclean!" the leper screams,
and all the people jump aside.

Now lepers should stay
a long way away
and not come close to clean men.
But this leper comes closer
and closer and closer,
and falls at Jesus' feet.

"My Lord! My Lord," he screams.
If You really want to do it,
You can make me clean."

Will Jesus use strange medicine
or some fancy magic stuff
to clean that unclean man?

No! He simply says, "Be clean!"
And without another word
the leprosy is gone!
It's gone!

Look again, my friends,
down by the city gate!
Are those the beggars Jesus loves
and other people hate?

Can you hear the beggars singing
about the cross-eyed dog
they say is king of their town?
They keep poking fun at anyone there
who walks around with his nose in the air
and thinks he's important somehow.

Can you hear them laughing now
as they hail their dog, Zigzog:

Oh, Zigzog, the blind man's dog!
You run just as straight as a frog.
You zog, we zig!
You zig, we zog!
You're Zigzog, the cross-eyed dog!

Oh, Zigzog, the cross-eyed clown!
You ought to wear Herod's crown.
He fools with rules!
You rule with fools!
You're king of the blind men in town.

King Herod went out for a jog.
You barked at him over a log.
He zogged, you zigged!
You zigged, he zogged!
And Herod fell flat in a bog.

Oh, Zigzog, the cross-eyed mutt!
Our priests have got into a rut.
We pay, they pray!
They pray, and we pay!
Your beggars just don't get their cut.

The high priest came asking for fees.
You barked and he fell on his knees.
He zogged, you zigged!
He zigged, you zogged!
Now the high priest is covered with fleas!

Look now!
As Jesus comes toward the gate,
the beggars stop their game.
They seem to know the reason
this Man called Jesus came.

He's talking to a beggar
who has always been quite blind.
"I am the Light of the world,"
said Jesus to the man.
"It's time to see, My friend."

Watch as Jesus kneels
and spits on the dusty ground.
He molds the dust into a paste
and rubs it very gently
on the blind man's eyes and face.

And can you hear Him saying,
"Go and wash your eyes
in that little pool nearby"?

Some people lead the blind man there,
though no one quite knows why.
For many men had come to wash
their hands and feet and sores
in that very same water,
but no one had been cured.

The blind man is kneeling
close to the edge of the pool
and washing the clay from his eyes.
Then faintly, so faintly,
he sees a flicker of light,
then another and another
until he sees great sheets of white,
flooding his eyes and soul
for the first time in his life.

Can you see him dancing now,
leaping, laughing, shouting,
"Jesus is a prophet, man!
Let's praise the Lord, and sing!"

Listen!
Can you hear the country dogs
howling, howling, howling?
And the women dressed in black,
wailing, wailing, wailing,
in a little town called Nain?

Can you see the funeral procession
coming slowly through the gate?
Instead of stepping aside
to let the funeral pass,
Jesus stops their sad trip
out to the empty grave.
But stopping a funeral procession
just isn't the way
for any good man to behave.
Now is it?

Jesus is speaking to one of the women
and asking her how it all happened.
"My husband is dead,"
the sad woman said,
"and now my only son has died."

Silently He touches the boards
where the dead boy is lying.

Then quietly Jesus says,
"Rise up! Rise up, young man!
It's time that you went home
and lived with your mother again."

Can you believe your eyes?
The boy is sitting up
as though he'd never been dead.
Yes! Yes!
The boy is talking and laughing
as though he'd never been dead.

As Jesus gives the boy
back to his mother again,
all the people shout,
"God has sent us a prophet!
A prophet! A prophet! Amen!
This Man is really Elijah.
He's risen from the dead.
These are the very miracles
that old Elijah did."

Yes, Jesus was a prophet,
and all His miracles were clues
that God had sent someone
to show us all His love.

For Jesus was the Son of God
and His love is a special clue
that He was doing God's purple puzzle
for you and you and you.

OTHER TITLES

SET I

WHEN GOD WAS ALL ALONE 56-1200
WHEN THE FIRST MAN CAME 56-1201
IN THE ENCHANTED GARDEN 56-1202
WHEN THE PURPLE WATERS CAME AGAIN 56-1203
IN THE LAND OF THE GREAT WHITE CASTLE 56-1204
WHEN LAUGHING BOY WAS BORN 56-1205
SET I LP RECORD 79-2200
SET I GIFT BOX (6 BOOKS, 1 RECORD) 56-1206

SET II

HOW TRICKY JACOB WAS TRICKED 56-1207
WHEN JACOB BURIED HIS TREASURE 56-1208
WHEN GOD TOLD US HIS NAME 56-1209
IS THAT GOD AT THE DOOR? 56-1210
IN THE MIDDLE OF A WILD CHASE 56-1211
THIS OLD MAN CALLED MOSES 56-1212
SET II LP RECORD 79-2201
SET II GIFT BOX (6 BOOKS, 1 RECORD) 56-1213

SET III

THE TROUBLE WITH TICKLE THE TIGER 56-1218
AT THE BATTLE OF JERICHO! HO! HO! 56-1219
GOD IS NOT A JACK-IN-A-BOX 56-1220
A LITTLE BOY WHO HAD A LITTLE FLING 56-1221
THE KING WHO WAS A CLOWN 56-1222
SING A SONG OF SOLOMON 56-1223
SET III LP RECORD 79-2202
SET III GIFT BOX (6 BOOKS, 1 RECORD) 56-1224

SET IV

ELIJAH AND THE BULL-GOD BAAL 56-1225
LONELY ELIJAH AND THE LITTLE PEOPLE 56-1226
WHEN ISAIAH SAW THE SIZZLING SERAPHIM 56-1227
A VOYAGE TO THE BOTTOM OF THE SEA 56-1228
WHEN JEREMIAH LEARNED A SECRET 56-1229
THE CLUMSY ANGEL AND THE NEW KING 56-1230
SET IV LP RECORD 79-2203
SET IV GIFT BOX (6 BOOKS, 1 RECORD) 56-1231

SET V

THE FIRST TRUE SUPER STAR 56-1242
A WILD YOUNG MAN CALLED JOHN 56-1243
THE DIRTY DEVIL AND THE CARPENTERS BOY 56-1244
WHEN JESUS DID HIS MIRACLES OF LOVE 56-1245
WHEN JESUS TOLD HIS PARABLES 56-1246
OLD ROCK THE FISHERMAN 56-1247
SET V LP RECORD 79-2204
SET V GIFT BOX 56-1248

SET VI

WONDER BREAD FROM A BOY'S LUNCH 56-1249
WHEN JESUS RODE IN THE PURPLE PUZZLE
   PARADE 56-1250
WHEN JESUS' FRIENDS BETRAYED HIM 56-1251
THE DEEP DARK DAY WHEN JESUS DIED 56-1252
DANCE, LITTLE ALLELU, WITH ME 56-1253
THE KEY TO THE PURPLE PUZZLE TREE 56-1254
SET VI LP RECORD 79-2205
SET VI GIFT BOX 56-1255

the PURPLE PUZZLE TREE